Bedtime Stories for Boys

BEDTIME STORIES FOR BOYS

First edition. March 14, 2023.

ISBN: 979-8215534502

Written by Liom Liom.

The brave knight

Once upon a time there was a brave knight named Jonas who lived in a faraway kingdom. Jonas was known for his bravery and unwavering courage in battle against enemies and monsters. One evening, as Jonas was making his way to the king's castle, he heard the loud roar of a dragon in the distance.

Without hesitation, Jonas set out to see what was going on. When he reached the dragon, he realized that it was just threatening a group of villagers. Jonas bravely confronted the dragon and fearlessly fought the fire-breathing monster.

But the dragon was too strong for Jonas and it seemed as if he would lose the fight. In desperation, Jonas called for help and suddenly he heard a voice telling him to find the courage in his heart and use his abilities to defeat the dragon.

Jonas realized that it was the king himself who was telling him to find courage and remembered that he always had to believe in himself. With a loud cry, Jonas attacked the dragon again and this time he fought with all his strength.

The fight lasted a long time, but finally Jonas managed to defeat the dragon. The villagers were saved and Jonas was hailed as a hero. But Jonas knew that without faith in himself and the help of the king, he would never have won the battle against the dragon.

And so Jonah went home and fell asleep happy, knowing that he would always find the courage in his heart to win any battle. The moral of this story is that you should always believe in yourself and use your abilities to overcome life's challenges.

THE ADVENTURE IN SPACE

Once upon a time, there was a little boy named Tom who had always dreamed of going into space and exploring the universe. One night he had a dream in which he was visited by a strange being who promised him an adventure in space.

Tom was excited and asked the being what he had to do to fly into space. The being replied that Tom had to use his faith in himself and his imagination to have the adventure.

And so Tom began his adventure in space. He closed his eyes and imagined himself flying in a spaceship through the vastness of space. Suddenly, he opened his eyes and was actually in a spaceship speeding through the universe.

Tom was thrilled and flew through the galaxies, visiting strange planets and meeting alien life forms. But when he visited a planet ruled by an evil tyrant, Tom was captured by his enemies.

Tom thought it was over and he would never return home. But then he remembered the creature's words and decided to use his faith in himself and his imagination to escape.

Tom imagined himself breaking free and flying out of the prison. And indeed, he was able to break free from the shackles and escape from the planet.

Tom returned home feeling proud of himself for overcoming his fears and mastering the adventure in space. The moral of this story is to always believe in yourself and use your imagination to achieve your dreams and overcome challenges. With courage and imagination, you can master any adventure in space or on Earth.

The secret agent

Once upon a time there was a little boy named Max who had always dreamed of being a secret agent. One day his dream came

true when he was recruited by a secret organization to fulfill an important mission.

Max was sent to a new city to find and return a stolen artifact. He had to penetrate the thieves' hideout and find the artifact without being discovered.

Max was nervous, but he remembered his training and his skills as an agent. He snuck into the thieves' hideout and found the artifact. But before he could escape, he was discovered.

Max had to flee and run through the city streets to escape the thieves. It was a wild chase in which Max did his best to escape from the thieves.

Finally, Max managed to bring back the artifact and catch the thieves. The organization was proud of him and he was hailed as a hero.

Max realized that it was not only important to have skills and training as an agent, but also to show courage and determination to accomplish his mission. The moral of this story is that you should always be ready to face challenges and do your best to succeed. With courage and determination, you can overcome any adventure as a secret agent.

THE DISCOVERY OF THE treasure

Once upon a time there was a little boy named Tim who dreamed of being an adventurer. One day he decided to go on a treasure hunt and set off into the forest where he believed a treasure was hidden.

Tim wandered through the forest, overcoming obstacles like streams and rocks to find the treasure. After some time, he found an old map that led him to an abandoned castle.

Tim entered the castle and found a hidden door that led to a secret room. There he discovered an old suitcase full of gold and jewels.

When he opened the suitcase, he was surprised by an evil robber who was also looking for the treasure. The robber threatened Tim and told him that he would not share the treasure.

But Tim was not intimidated. He remembered the adventures he had had in his imagination and used his imagination to develop a strategy.

Tim lured the robber into a room and closed the door. Then he called the police to arrest the robber.

Tim became a hero and got to keep the treasure. But he also realized that the treasure was not the most important thing. The real reward was that he had overcome his fears and mastered his adventure.

The moral of this story is that adventures are not just about finding treasure, but also about showing courage and determination to overcome challenges. With imagination and determination, you can master any adventure and find your own treasure.

The superhero day

It was a sunny day and little boy Max had a special adventure planned: He was going to be a superhero! He put on his favorite superhero mask and set out to fulfill his mission.

Max wanted to spend the day doing good and helping people in need. He rescued a cat from a tree, helped an old lady who dropped her grocery bags, and gave a child who dropped his ice cream his own ice cream.

But when he saw a man being robbed, he decided to intervene. He put on his mask and charged to stop the robber.

It was an exciting fight between Max and the robber. Max fought bravely and decisively and finally managed to overpower the robber. The police came and arrested the robber.

Max was celebrated as a hero and felt great. However, he also realized that each of us can be superheroes by helping others and doing good.

The moral of this story is that everyone has the power to be a superhero by helping others and doing good. You don't need superpowers to be a hero. It is enough to be kind, helpful and brave. You can be a superhero every day!

SAVING THE DINOSAUR

It was a sunny day and the little boy Tom was exploring in the forest. Suddenly he heard a loud roar and followed the sound. As he got closer, he saw a dinosaur caught in a thorn bush.

Tom knew he had to help. He remembered his favorite story about a dinosaur being rescued and decided he would try too.

Tom cautiously approached the dinosaur and noticed that it had a deep cut on its paw. He felt that he could not leave the dinosaur alone and decided to rescue it.

He tied his scarf around the dinosaur's wound and helped it get out of the thorn bush. The dinosaur roared with joy and thanked Tom for his help.

But suddenly they noticed that a pack of hungry wolves was chasing the dinosaur. Tom realized that they had to act quickly to save the dinosaur.

Tom led the dinosaur to a cave he had found in another story and helped it hide. The wolves arrived and looked for the dinosaur, but they couldn't find him.

Tom and the dinosaur were safe and the dinosaur thanked Tom again for his help.

The moral of this story is that it is important to help others, even if it is unexpected and you are scared. You can always do something to help others in need and it can change the lives of others. Tom had the courage to help a dinosaur in need and was able to save him.

THE SORCERER'S APPRENTICE

Once upon a time there was a little boy named Felix who dreamed of being a magician. He wanted to learn magic tricks and impress his friends.

One day, Felix decided to make his dream come true and find a real magic wand. He set off into the forest and came across a mysterious hut. When he opened the door, he found an old magic wand on the table.

Felix knew he couldn't just play around with the wand, so he asked for help from his favorite magic book. But unfortunately, Felix couldn't understand the book because it was written in a foreign language.

Felix thought that he could still try, thinking that the book would help him learn magic tricks. He tried to wave the magic wand, but nothing happened.

Felix didn't give up and kept trying until he accidentally cast an evil spell and shrouded the cottage in darkness. Suddenly, the old wand came alive and threatened to destroy everything.

Felix was distraught and didn't know how to stop the wand. But then he remembered his parents' advice that you should always ask for help when you are in trouble.

He prayed to God and asked for help. Suddenly, the wand slowed down and weakened until it finally disappeared.

Felix learned an important lesson: that it is not good to do things you don't understand, and that it is always better to ask for help when you are in trouble.

The moral of this story is that you should never get into trouble on your own, especially when it comes to things you don't understand. It is important to ask for help when you are stuck. That's the only way to learn and grow.

THE MIRACLE OF THE Rainbow

Once upon a time there was a little boy named Luke who loved to play outside and have adventures. One day, while walking through the forest, he noticed a beautiful rainbow in the sky.

Luke was fascinated by the bright colors and was determined to find out where the rainbow ended. So he followed it, on and on, until he finally arrived at the foot of a mountain.

There he met an old man who explained to him that at the top of the mountain there was a magical well that dyed the water in all the colors of the rainbow. The old man also told him that only someone who had a very strong connection to the rainbow would be able to drink the water from the well and thereby experience the miracle of the rainbow.

Luke was eager to experience the miracle of the rainbow and decided to climb the mountain. It was an arduous journey, full of obstacles and dangers. But Luke did not give up and fought his way through.

Finally, he reached the top of the mountain and found the magic well. He drank the water and was flooded with incredible energy. He could suddenly do things he had never thought possible before.

Luke understood that the rainbow is not only beautiful to look at, but also has a powerful force. He learned that you can achieve what you really want through perseverance, courage and willpower. You should never give up and always believe in your dreams.

From that day on, Luke was a different boy. He believed in the miracle of the rainbow and that everything is possible if you only believe in it and work hard for it. He told his story to many people and inspired them to make their own dreams come true.

The moral of this story is that we all have a strong connection to the miracle of the rainbow. It is important to believe in our dreams, pursue them and not get discouraged. If we work hard and don't get discouraged, we can achieve anything we can imagine.

THE RIDDLES OF THE Lost Temple

Once upon a time there was a boy named Max who was a great adventurer. One day he heard about a lost temple hidden deep in the jungle. It was said that the temple was full of treasures and secrets that had been hidden for centuries.

Max was intrigued by this story and decided to find the temple. With his equipment and courage, he set out into the jungle.

The search was difficult and dangerous, but Max did not give up. Finally, he found the temple, but the entrance was blocked. Max had to solve a series of riddles to enter the temple.

Each time Max solved a puzzle, a new area of the temple opened up to him. But the puzzles became more and more difficult and complex, and Max began to doubt whether he would ever enter the temple.

Finally, Max came across the most difficult puzzle of all. He spent hours trying to solve it, but got nowhere. Max was devastated and ready to give up when a flash of inspiration came to him.

He realized that he couldn't solve the puzzle on his own, and that he needed help. He remembered his friends who had always helped him when he was in trouble. He called them and asked for their help.

Together they worked on the puzzle and finally they found the solution. The temple opened and Max entered. He found a treasury full of gold and jewels.

But Max realized that the real treasure was having solved the riddle together with his friends. He learned that sometimes it is okay to ask for help and that true friendship is priceless.

The moral of the story is that sometimes you need help to solve difficult puzzles. It's important to ask friends and family for support when you're in trouble. And that the real treasure is not always what you see at first glance, but is often what you learn along the way and who helps you.

THE PIRATE KING

Once upon a time there was a little boy named Tim who had always dreamed of adventures and pirates. One night he had a strange dream in which he was on a big ship and searching for a secret treasure. When he woke up, he was still fascinated by this dream.

Tim decided to go on an adventure and find the treasure. He packed a few things, like a map, a flashlight and a magnifying glass. Then he set off to the harbor to find a ship.

After searching for a while, Tim finally found an old but powerful ship that was steered by an old man. The man was a famous pirate king who had been at sea for many years and had found many treasures. Tim asked him if he could accompany him on his search for the secret treasure.

The pirate king was skeptical at first, but when he saw the determination in Tim's eyes, he finally agreed. Together they sailed across the vast sea, overcoming dangerous currents and storms, until they finally came across a deserted island.

On the island they found an ancient temple surrounded by jungle. There were many riddles and traps there, but Tintin and the Pirate King worked together and solved them one by one. Finally, they found the treasure, which consisted of precious gems and gold coins.

But on the way back they were attacked by other pirates who claimed the treasure for themselves. In a fierce battle, Tintin and the pirate king fought back and finally escaped. On their ship, they sailed back to their hometown and divided the treasure fairly.

Tintin realized that the adventure was not just about the treasure, but also about the friendship he had made with the pirate king. He had learned that even in difficult situations, you have to stick together to achieve a goal.

And so Tim fell asleep with a smile on his face and dreamed of more adventures on the high seas.

The hunt for the secret of the unicorn

Once upon a time there was a little boy named Tim who wanted nothing more than to have an adventure. One day he heard about a secret unicorn that supposedly lived in the mountains. No one knew exactly where to find it or if it even really existed, but Tim was determined to find it.

So he set out and crossed forests, crossed rivers and climbed steep mountains. Finally, he reached a deep forest where he met a group of travelers who were also looking for the unicorn. The travelers were all very friendly and decided to accept Tim into their group.

Together they crossed the forest and finally reached a deep river. To get to the other side, they had to use an old, crumbling boat. When they were in the middle of the river, the boat suddenly broke apart and the travelers and Tim were thrown into the water.

They swam to shore and found that their map and equipment had been lost in the water. But Tim did not give up. He suggested that they keep going and memorize the way.

Day and night they continued to wander until they finally reached an ancient temple. In the center of the temple stood a majestic unicorn. Tintin and the travelers cautiously approached the unicorn and realized it was following them when they decided to help it.

The unicorn had gotten into trouble when it was kidnapped by an evil wizard. But Tintin and his friends were brave and fought the wizard until he finally released the unicorn.

The unicorn was grateful and Tintin and his friends were allowed to ride it. Together they flew through the sky and had many adventures.

And when Tim finally returned home, he had become a different boy. He had learned that it takes courage, perseverance, and friendship to have adventures. And he knew that as long as he had these qualities in him, he would have adventures for the rest of his life.

THE MAGIC LAMP

Once upon a time, there was a little boy named Ali who discovered an old lamp at a flea market. The lamp was dusty and seemed to have been forgotten for years. Ali bought it for just one cent and took it home.

As he cleaned the lamp, Ali noticed that there was a small note attached to it that said, "Rub me three times and your wish will come true." Ali was curious and decided to rub the lamp.

To his surprise, a tall, muscular man with a turban cap on his head appeared. "I am your Genie and I will grant you three wishes," the man said.

Ali could not believe his eyes. He had heard that there were djinn in stories like Aladdin and the Magic Lamp, but he had never thought he would meet one himself.

"Oh, I wish I could fly like a bird," Ali said.

Immediately, the djinn transformed Ali into a little bird and they flew through the clouds together.

"This is amazing!" exclaimed Ali as they soared in the clouds.

"That was your first wish, do you have any others?" asked the Djinni.

Ali thought about it and finally said, "I wish for all my friends to be happy and for their wishes to come true."

Suddenly all his friends appeared and each of them had his own djinni. The friends told Ali that they had to rub themselves to activate their djinn.

Ali was happy that he could help his friends make their dreams come true. They played and laughed together and had a wonderful time.

But then Ali realized that he had forgotten to make his last wish.

"I wish I never forget what is really important again," Ali said.

The djinn smiled and said, "Your wish is granted. But remember, Ali, that the most important thing in life is not always what you wish for. It's the people around you and the memories you share with them."

Ali nodded and thanked the Genie for granting his wishes. He knew now that he would always keep the lamp and remember the Djinni's words. For life is the greatest miracle there is.

THE JOURNEY TO THE moon

Once upon a time there was a little boy named Max who dreamed of traveling to the moon. He would stare up at the sky every night and wonder what it would be like to be on that faraway planet. One day, he decided he had enough just dreaming about it - he would actually go there!

Max began studying everything he could find about rockets and space travel. He built models of rockets and even had his own little control room in his room. His parents were amazed at his interest, but supported him and helped him learn everything he needed to start his journey to the moon.

One night, as Max lay in bed staring up at the sky again, he saw a strange string of lights in the distance. It was moving fast and flying directly toward him. As the object got closer, Max realized it was a spaceship! The door opened and a small, green alien climbed out.

"Come with me, Max!" said the alien. "I'll take you to the moon!"

Max didn't hesitate and got into the spaceship. The rocket shot into the sky and soon they were on their way to the moon.

On the journey, Max learned a lot from the alien, who showed him how to put on a spacesuit and how to live in zero gravity. Finally, they landed on the moon and Max was completely amazed. He was bouncing and jumping around on the surface of the moon when suddenly he heard a noise.

He followed the sound and discovered a group of small, friendly creatures living on the moon. They showed him their home and Max was fascinated by all the amazing things they had.

When it was time to go back to Earth, Max was sad to leave the moon, but he knew he would always have a special connection to this distant planet. He returned home and told everyone about his incredible journey to the moon.

Max had learned that it's important to have dreams and work hard to achieve them. Sometimes dreams can even come true if you work hard enough at it and are willing to take risks. But he had also learned that it is important to be grateful for the things you have and to appreciate the wonderful world around you.

THE SOCCER STAR

Once upon a time, there was a little boy named Tim. He was a big soccer fan and dreamed of one day becoming a famous soccer player himself.

One day, Tim received an invitation to try out for the local soccer club. He was excited and practiced hard to prepare for the training.

When he finally arrived at the tryout, there were many other talented boys there. They played hard and tried their best to get on the team.

Tim fought hard and performed great on the court. But then he tripped and hurt himself. His leg hurt so much that he could not continue playing.

Disappointed, Tim returned home and was sad that he couldn't finish the tryout.

But then he remembered his father's words, "Winners are not those who never fail, but those who never give up."

Tim decided to never give up and keep working hard to achieve his goal.

And so he practiced every day and eventually became so good that he was accepted into the soccer team. He played hard and showed team spirit, helping his teammates get better.

At the end of the season, Tim's team won the finals and he was named the game's most valuable player.

Tim learned that hard training, determination and teamwork can lead to success. And he became a great soccer player who always believed in his dreams and never gave up.

THE DANGEROUS DRAGON

Once upon a time there was a little boy named Tim who dreamed of a brave story. One night, as he slept, he had a dream in which he was drawn into a fantasy world full of dragons and adventure.

Tim was on an island that was ruled by a giant dragon. The dragon was dangerous and tyrannical and had terrified the islanders. Tim decided to put an end to the dragon and save the islanders.

With courage and determination, Tim set out for Dragon Mountain, where the dragon lived. He climbed up the steep mountain and finally reached the cave where the dragon lived. The dragon was not pleased to see Tim and tried to destroy him. Tim ran and jumped to avoid the dragon's fire breath.

Suddenly, Tim fell into a pit that he had not seen coming. There he discovered a sword that looked like it had been there for centuries. Tim took the sword and swung it at the dragon. With each blow he weakened the dragon until it was finally defeated.

The islanders were relieved and thanked Tim for his bravery. Tim had learned that with courage and determination, you can overcome any challenge. He returned to his bed, but he knew that he would continue to have adventures in his dreams.

The moral of this story is that it takes courage and determination to overcome obstacles and achieve your goals. If you believe in yourself and work hard, you can accomplish anything you set your mind to.

THE DETECTIVE AND THE Stolen Treasure

Once upon a time there was a little boy named Tim who dreamed of becoming a famous detective. One day he got the chance to realize his dream when the treasure of the famous museum of the city was stolen.

Tim did not hesitate and immediately started searching for the stolen treasure. He examined the crime scene evidence and found that the thief had to be a talented burglar. Tim worked tirelessly to find any clue that might lead him to the thief.

One night, Tim heard a noise in the museum and decided to investigate. He crept quietly through the dark corridors and saw a shadow moving through the galleries. He followed the shadow and saw the thief who had the stolen treasure in a bag.

Tim knew he had to confront the thief, but he was alone and the thief was much bigger and stronger than him. Tim hesitated for a moment, but then he remembered what he had learned in his favorite detective stories: that courage and determination always lead to success.

Tim used his courage and jumped toward the thief. The thief was surprised and fought Tim, but Tim did not give up and managed to get back the bag with the stolen treasure.

The next day, Tim was praised by the police for his courage and determination. Not only had he found the stolen treasure, but he had also caught the thief. Tim was happy and proud of himself and knew that he had achieved his dream of becoming a famous detective.

The moral of this story is that courage and determination are the keys to success. You have to be willing to take risks to achieve what you want.

The day at the zoo

It was a sunny day and Tom was excited because his family had decided to spend the day at the zoo. Tom loved animals and couldn't wait to see all the different species.

When they arrived at the entrance, Tom could see the excitement sparkling in his eyes. He and his family started walking from one enclosure to the next, admiring all the animals, from elephants to monkeys and lions. But then they reached the giraffe enclosure.

Tom was fascinated by the giraffes' long legs and neck, and he decided to give them some grass, which he picked from a nearby tree. He put his hand through the bars of the enclosure and held up the grass. Suddenly, a giraffe came closer and started eating the grass from Tom's hand. Tom was so happy that he forgot to watch where he was stepping, and suddenly he tripped and fell into the enclosure!

Tom was lucky because the giraffes were gentle animals and the one that ate the grass from Tom's hand licked his face and helped him stand up. But then Tom realized he was in a tough spot - he was locked in the giraffe enclosure!

The giraffes seemed to notice this too and came closer to help him. They gently pushed him toward the bars and Tom was finally able to squeeze through. He landed on the other side where his family was anxiously waiting for him.

Tom was relieved to be rescued, but he also learned an important lesson: always watch where you step and don't put yourself in dangerous situations. The giraffes were his salvation, but he knew he would be more careful in the future. Together they continued to walk through the zoo and had many more adventures and learned even more important lessons. And so their day at the zoo ended with a lot of fun and a new experience for Tom.

THE TIME MACHINE

Once upon a time, there was a little boy named Max who was passionate about all things technical and scientific. One day, he found an old box in his grandfather's attic that was labeled with dusty characters. When Max opened the box, he discovered a strange machine with lots of levers and buttons that looked like a time machine.

Max could hardly believe it! He had read a lot about time travel and was excited about the idea of traveling into the past or future. He was eager to try out whether the machine would work. So he put the time machine on the floor and pressed the button labeled "Start."

Suddenly, Max was surrounded by a bright light and he felt himself being catapulted through time. He finally landed in a strange world he had never seen before. It was a world full of colors and creatures that looked like beings from another dimension.

Max decided to explore this strange world and met many friendly creatures who helped him find his way around. But soon he also noticed a dark threat: an evil tyrant wanted to rule this world and enslave all creatures. Max decided to act and helped the creatures to defend themselves against the tyrant.

An epic battle ensued between Max and the tyrant, but in the end Max was able to achieve victory and free the creatures. With a grin on his face, Max finally returned to the present filled with pride and adventure.

Max had learned an important lesson: it pays to take risks and be brave. Sometimes you can achieve great things and change the lives of others.

The Enchanted Castle

Once upon a time there was a little boy named Tim who was fascinated by stories about knights and castles. One day he decided to go exploring and find an enchanted castle he had heard about in an old legend.

He wandered for hours through the forest until he finally spotted a tower in the distance. Tim was excited and ran there as fast as he could. When he reached the castle, he discovered a rusted gate that was half open. He slipped inside and began to explore.

But suddenly he heard a voice ordering him to leave immediately. Tim was startled to realize that the castle was enchanted and the spirit of the old knight still lived there.

The knight's spirit explained to Tim that he was trapped in the castle and would only release him if he helped him find a secret treasure. Tim was brave and agreed.

Together they walked through the dark corridors and searched for the treasure. They encountered many obstacles and had to fight scary creatures guarding the treasure.

But Tim did not give up and fought bravely. Finally, they reached the treasure and the knight's spirit was free. In return, he gave Tim a magic coin that would help him be brave in difficult situations.

Tim returned home and was proud of his adventures. He realized that courage and determination helped him to overcome any challenge. From that day on, he always carried the magic coin with him and always remembered that he could be brave if he really wanted to be.

THE GREAT STORM

Once upon a time, there was a little boy named Tim who was on vacation at the beach with his parents and his little brother Max. They had been looking forward to a beautiful sunset when suddenly the sky got darker and darker. The clouds gathered and it began to storm.

Tim and his family ran back to their beach house to get to safety. But the storm became more and more violent. The house shook and the windows rattled in the wind. Tim was afraid the house would collapse.

But then he remembered his father, who had once told him how important it is to keep a cool head in difficult situations and to help each other. So he called his little brother and parents together and suggested that they leave the house and take refuge in a more stable building.

Together, they ran to the nearby hotel, where they encountered other guests who were also seeking shelter. The hotel staff tried to get all the guests to safety while the storm continued to rage outside.

It was a long and frightening night, but the storm finally calmed down the next morning. Tim and his family were relieved to be safe and decided to continue their vacation.

But Tim had learned from the storm the importance of staying calm and helping each other in difficult situations. He was proud of himself for keeping his cool and helping his family get to safety.

As they walked along the beach and saw the devastation of the storm, they decided to help together and clean up the beach. Tim knew that together they could make a big difference and that it was important to stand together in difficult times.

So their vacation ended differently than planned, but Tim had learned something much more important: that cohesion and help are the most important things in difficult times.

THE DISCOVERY OF THE underwater world

Once upon a time there was a boy named Tim who lived by the sea. He was always fascinated by the beauty of the ocean and dreamed of one day discovering the underwater world. One day he decided to go on an adventure and explore the secrets of the sea.

Equipped with his wetsuit and diving gear, Tim set off into the sea. He swam through the clear water and saw fish of all colors and sizes, coral reefs and even turtles.

But suddenly, Tim noticed that he was moving deeper and deeper into the sea and realized that he didn't know how to get back. But instead of panicking, he remembered the teachings of his father, who had always told him to stay calm and level-headed in dangerous situations.

So Tim swam on and on until he finally came across a beautiful underwater cave. He swam into it and could hardly believe his luck when he made an incredible discovery: a sunken city that no one had ever seen before!

Tim was so excited that he quickly forgot about going back and focused on discovering the city. But when he finally wanted to return, he noticed that a storm had announced itself. The waves were higher than him and the wind was getting stronger.

Tim knew he had to act quickly now to get to safety. He swam as fast as he could, but the storm was too strong. He couldn't swim any further and had to grab onto a rock.

However, Tim did not give up. He remembered what his father had taught him and found the strength and courage to face the storm. He swam with all his might and finally reached the shore where his family was waiting for him.

Tim told his family about his incredible discovery and about his struggle against the storm. His family was proud of him and admired his bravery and courage.

And Tim learned an important lesson: if you face your fears and remain calm and level-headed, you can overcome any challenge and even discover unexpected treasures.

THE FLIGHT TO THE NORTH Pole

It was a beautiful day at the airport. The sun was shining and the sky was bright blue. At the terminal, many passengers were waiting for their flights. But there was one group of passengers who were especially happy. They were on their way to a special adventure: a flight to the North Pole.

The group consisted of five children and their parents. The children were all between six and eight years old and were more excited than ever. They had learned from school about the importance of taking care of our environment and using clean energy sources. So they had decided to visit the North Pole and learn more about renewable energy.

When they finally sat in the plane and took off, the children couldn't take their eyes off the clouds and mountains below them. It was an exciting feeling to be so high in the air. But soon the excitement had died down and everyone was ready to lie down and take a nap.

But suddenly the plane was caught in a violent storm. The children and their parents were startled and clung to each other. The captain immediately announced that everyone should fasten their seat belts and stand by. The plane was shaken and the passengers felt it being tossed back and forth again and again.

After some time, when the storm subsided, the rattle of the turbines could be heard again and the plane was flying steadily. But it soon became apparent that the plane had sustained damage. The captain explained that they had to make an emergency landing because the plane could no longer fly safely.

The passengers were frightened, but also relieved that they could land safely. They got off the plane and discovered that they had landed in the middle of nowhere. But they were not discouraged and began to look around.

In the process, they discovered an amazing thing: a huge wind turbine standing in the middle of the snow. The children were fascinated and were eager to learn more about it. So they decided to explore the area and learn more about renewable energy.

They discovered more wind turbines and learned how important it is to use clean energy sources to protect our environment. The children were so inspired that they decided to start a project at their school to encourage other children to learn more about renewable energy and become involved in protecting the environment.

At the end of the trip, the children and their parents were grateful for the adventure and the chance to learn about the importance of renewable energy. They had a lot of fun and had learned a valuable lesson: that it is important to take care of our environment and protect our planet.

THE LOST SNOWMAN

It was just before Christmas and overnight it had snowed. Little Tom was very excited and after breakfast he rushed into the garden to build a snowman. Together with his father he formed a big snowball and a smaller one for the head. Tom also got twigs for the arms and stones for the eyes and mouth. The snowman looked just perfect!

But the next morning the snowman was gone. Tom and his father searched in the garden and also asked the neighbors, but no one had seen the snowman. Tom was heartbroken and his father promised him that they would find the snowman together.

They started their search in the neighbor's garden, where they had last seen the snowman. But suddenly they heard a strange noise and followed him to a nearby forest. There they discovered a group of squirrels who were busy dragging the snowman into their den.

Tom and his father tracked the squirrels to their den and saw that they had placed the snowman on a spot that was illuminated by the sun. The squirrels had taken the snowman because they thought it was a lost friend and wanted to save it. Tom and his father were touched by the care of the little animals.

When they returned home, Tom and his father built a new snowman, but this time they made it together with the squirrels. They put it in a spot in the garden where everyone could see it. Tom learned that it is important to pay attention to other animals and their needs, and that cooperation and friendship are the keys to a happy life.

And so the snowman remained a sign of friendship between people and animals, rebuilt every year at winter time.

The Adventures of Tom Müller

Once upon a time there was a boy named Tom Müller. Tom was an adventurous boy who was always looking for new challenges. One day he decided to explore the nearby forest.

As he was wandering through the forest, he suddenly heard a strange noise. It sounded like the cracking of branches. Tom followed the sound and saw a big bear stuck in a thorn bush. The bear had hurt itself and could not move.

Tom knew he had to help the bear. He approached the bear carefully and saw that its paw was caught in a thorn bush. Tom didn't hesitate for long and began to remove the thorn bush with a stick. It took a while, but finally he managed to free the bear.

When the bear was free, he looked at Tom with a grateful look. Tom knew that he now had a responsibility to the bear. He decided to help the bear find his family. He wondered how he could do that and decided to continue exploring the forest.

Tom wandered through the forest for hours and saw many animals he had never seen before. Suddenly he heard a noise that sounded like a roar. He followed the sound and found a group of wolves standing around an injured wolf.

Tom knew he had to help. He began to treat the injured wolf and noticed that it had many injuries. He knew he could not leave the wolf alone and decided to care for him until he was well again.

After a few days, Tom had helped the injured wolf recover. The wolf was so grateful that he offered to lead Tom to a secret lair where many lost animals lived.

Tom followed the wolf to the secret hiding place and was surprised to see how many lost animals lived there. They were all grateful for Tom's help and decided to help him find the bear.

Tom and the bear were finally reunited and Tom was happy to see that the bear had finally found his family. Tom knew it was important to help animals in need, and he was proud that he had helped.

The moral of the story is that it is important to help others and to be attentive to the needs of animals. Sometimes you can also make surprising friends by helping others.

THE DISCOVERY OF THE pyramids

Once upon a time there was a little boy named Max who was always fascinated by adventures and discoveries. One day he received an invitation from his grandfather, who lived in Egypt, to visit the pyramids.

Max was excited and couldn't wait to see the mysterious structures. When he finally got there, his grandfather told him about the legend of a hidden treasure in one of the pyramids. Max was thrilled and decided to find the treasure.

Together with his grandfather, he set out for the pyramid that contained the treasure. Along the way, they encountered many challenges and dangers, such as a sandstorm and dangerous scorpions. But Max and his grandfather did not give up and fought their way bravely.

Finally, they reached the pyramid and began to explore it. They encountered many riddles and mysteries that they had to solve in order to move forward. But Max and his grandfather were smart and eventually found the hidden treasure.

When they found the treasure, they realized that it wasn't about the money or the riches, but about the adventure and friendship they had found on their journey. They realized that the adventure they had shared together was worth more than any treasure.

Max returned home, but he never forgot what he had learned. He knew that life was full of challenges and adventures, but he also knew that he could do anything if he just worked hard enough and believed in himself.

Saving the planet

Once upon a time there was a boy named Max who loved to look up at the sky and watch the stars. He dreamed of one day flying into space and discovering strange planets. One night, when Max was looking at the sky again, he noticed something strange: the planet Earth was covered by dark clouds and looked sad.

Max decided to find out what was going on. He ran to his computer and googled "planet earth threatened." What he found shocked him: the planet was in danger from climate change and something urgently needed to be done to save it.

Max thought long and hard about how he could help. Finally, he had an idea: he would build a rocket to fly into space and find a way to save the planet. Max worked hard on his plan and was finally able to build his own rocket.

When Max arrived in space, he saw that the planet was in terrible condition. There was trash everywhere and the air was thicker than ever. Max was not discouraged, however. He decided that he would not give up on the planet and started looking for solutions.

He found a group of alien beings who helped him build a machine that could clean the air. Together with the aliens, Max cleaned the air and collected the garbage to save the planet.

When Max returned to Earth, he saw that the planet was clean and fresh again. People were grateful for his work and called him the hero who had saved the planet.

Max was proud of his accomplishment, but he also knew that it was important to protect the planet in the future. He began to tell others about the importance of protecting the planet and how everyone could contribute.

So Max learned that even a little boy like him can change the world if he works hard and believes in what he is doing. And so Max decided to become an environmental activist and continue to work to protect the planet.

THE DAY AT THE AMUSEMENT park

It was a sunny day and Tim was excited. Today he would go to the amusement park with his family. He had planned weeks in advance which attractions he really wanted to try. When they arrived, Tim ran to the entrance to scan the map and get on his way.

The family started with the slower rides and then made their way to the roller coasters. Tim was a little nervous, but he wanted to be brave and give it a try. As they rode the roller coaster, Tim felt like he was flying. It was so exciting that he kept screaming and laughing on the ride.

But suddenly they heard an announcement, "Attention, we have a disturbance on the roller coaster. Please remain calm and in your seats until we can resolve the situation."

The family became nervous, but Tim tried to remain calm. Park staff worked hard to fix the problem and eventually they were all able to get off the ride safely.

After the incident was fixed, they decided to take a break and seek refreshments. On the way to the snack bar, Tim spotted a frightened boy who was lost and couldn't find his parents. Tim felt sorry for him and decided to help him.

He calmed the boy down and together they searched for his parents. After some time, they finally found them. The parents were overjoyed to see their son again and thanked Tim for his help.

At the end of the day, as they walked back to their car, Tim felt a sense of satisfaction. Not only had he had a great time at the amusement park, but he had helped others. He realized that it's not always about his own enjoyment, but that helping others can be very fulfilling as well.

The treasure hunt on the beach

It was a sunny day on the beach when a couple of boys decided to go on a treasure hunt. The sun was shining, the waves were crashing and the seagulls were screeching in the sky. The friends got ready and put on their treasure hunting gear: Binoculars, shovels, metal detectors and maps.

They followed the instructions on the map and set off. They dug deep holes in the sand and searched for buried treasure. They searched for hours, but it seemed they would find nothing. The sun began to set and they knew they would have to leave soon. But they didn't give up and kept searching.

Finally, one of the boys found something metallic in the sand. They pondered what it could be. Was it an old key? Or a coin? They grabbed the shovel and began to uncover the object. After a few minutes of effort, they revealed an old chest.

The boys' eyes widened with excitement. They opened the chest and found a pile of gold coins, jewels and other treasures inside. They cheered and hugged each other, and their faces beamed with joy.

But when they turned around, they saw a man in dirty clothes coming toward them. The man grabbed the chest and ran away. The boys were horrified and sad that the man had stolen their treasure. They decided to chase after him.

The boys ran after the man and finally stopped him. They demanded that the man give them back their treasure. The man was surprised by the boys' determination and finally gave in. He returned the chest to them and apologized to them.

The boys learned an important lesson about friendship and cohesion that day. They realized that they can accomplish anything if they work together and never give up. At the end of the day, the boys returned home happy and proud and shared their adventures with their families and friends.

THE BRAVE FIREMAN

It was a hot summer day and the sun was burning from the sky. Most kids spent their time at the beach or splashing around in the pool, but not Tim. Tim had dreamed of being a firefighter for years. When he heard there was an open house at the local fire department, he was eager to attend.

When he got there, there were already lots of people there and the firefighters were showing off their impressive vehicles and equipment. Tim was quite excited when he saw the big turntable ladder and the firemen explained to him how it worked. Suddenly, the peace was interrupted when the alarm went off. There was a fire in the nearby forest and the firemen had to act quickly.

Tim was excited and wanted to help, but he knew he was too young to go. He saw the firefighters quickly put on their protective gear and jump into the fire trucks. Tim followed them on his bike and saw them hurry to the fire scene.

By the time they arrived, the fire was out of control and flames were leaping high into the sky. The firefighters bravely fought the flames and eventually managed to put out the fire.

Tim was impressed by the bravery of the firefighters and now knew that he wanted to be one of them. He decided to work hard every day and learn everything he could to become a firefighter one day.

The moral of the story is that we should all pursue our dreams and work hard to achieve our goals. Bravery and courage are also important qualities we should all have to help others in need.

THE FIGHT AGAINST THE monster

Once upon a time there was a little boy named Max who dreamed of being a heroic fighter. One night, when Max was fast asleep, he suddenly woke up to a loud thunder. He jumped out of bed and ran to his window to see what was going on. In the distance he could see a horrible monster terrorizing the city and destroying everything around him.

Max knew he had to help. He quickly got dressed and ran towards the monster. As he got closer, he could feel his legs shaking and his heart beating fast. But he knew he had to be brave. He drew his sword, which he had carved from a piece of wood, and bravely walked toward the monster.

The monster was huge and dangerous, but Max did not give up. He fought the monster while relying on his speed and skill to dodge it. The monster was strong and did not make it easy for him, but Max did not give up. He continued to fight and did everything he could to defeat the monster.

Then an idea came to him. He remembered the story of David and Goliath from the Bible, and decided to use the stone he had in his pocket. He aimed accurately and threw the stone at the monster. The stone hit the monster right in the eye and the monster fell to the ground.

Max was happy and proud of himself. He had defeated the monster and saved the town. He was hailed as a hero by all the people in the town.

The moral of the story is that you should always be brave and never give up, even when facing a seemingly invincible enemy. One should always remember one's strengths and talents and do everything to defend what is good.

THE INVENTION OF THE airplane

Once upon a time, there was a little boy named Max who had always dreamed of flying. He was fascinated by birds and airplanes and was dying to know how to fly through the air.

One day, Max heard about a man named Wilbur Wright who, along with his brother Orville, had invented the airplane. Max was excited and decided to learn more about the Wright brothers and their invention.

He visited the library and read everything he could find about airplanes. Finally, he had enough knowledge and decided to build his own plane. He grabbed some materials and started to construct his plane.

It was harder than expected, but Max didn't give up. Finally, his plane was ready for the test flight. He ran as fast as he could and jumped into his plane. It started to wobble and sway, but finally it took off!

Max felt as free as a bird and enjoyed the ride in his homemade plane. He flew over forests, mountains and oceans and saw the world from a whole new perspective.

When he finally returned to earth, Max knew that if he just worked hard enough and never gave up, he could make his dreams come true.

The moral of the story is that you can achieve anything you set your mind to if you work hard and never give up.

THE SECRET CAVE

Once upon a time there was a little boy named Max who was very adventurous and always looking for new adventures. One day he was playing in the forest with his friends when he discovered a strange cave. The cave was covered with leaves and branches, and Max couldn't resist exploring what was hiding inside.

He crept into the cave and quickly discovered that it was a secret cave that no one knew about. It was dark and cold in the cave, but Max could see the light from outside and decided to go deeper in.

As he went deeper into the cave, he heard a strange noise. It sounded like scratching or tapping. Max became curious and followed the sound to an old door. He gently pushed against it and it opened.

Behind the door was a secret laboratory full of devices and machines. Max couldn't believe it and started exploring the machines. He found a machine that seemed to be a time machine. He read the instructions and decided to try it out.

Max got into the time machine and pressed the button. The machine began to whir and glow, and suddenly Max was gone. He found himself in another time, thousands of years ago.

He landed in a world full of dinosaurs and other strange creatures. Max was excited and thrilled, but he also realized that he was in danger. He had to find a way to get back to his own time before it was too late.

Max set out and explored the area. He met friendly dinosaurs who helped him and also had to fight dangerous predators. After many adventures, he finally found a way back to his own time.

When he returned, he was relieved to be back home, but he also missed the adventures and friends he had made in the past. He realized that life is full of adventures and opportunities if you are just brave enough to take them.

Max returned to the secret cave and wrote down all his adventures. He decided to always be brave in the future and to stay on the lookout for new adventures, no matter where they would take him. And so Max lived his life full of adventures and discoveries, encouraging others to do the same.

THE CIRCUS COMES TO town

It was a sunny day in the small town on the edge of the forest. The birds were chirping happily and the children were playing in the streets. Suddenly they heard a loud rumbling and clattering. The circus had arrived in town! All the children ran excitedly to the circus grounds to see what was happening.

When they arrived, they saw a large circus ring and many tents housing the circus performers and animals. Some of the children watched in fascination as the circus performers performed breathtaking feats, while others excitedly roamed the tents looking at the animals.

Suddenly, a little boy named Max noticed a circus clown standing sadly in the corner. Max, who was brave and curious, went to him and asked, "What's wrong, clown? Why are you so sad?"

The clown told him that he had lost his magic hat, which he needed for his magic tricks. Without it, he could no longer perform his tricks and was very afraid of losing his job.

Max, wanting to help, said, "I will find your hat and bring it back!" The clown was overjoyed and gave him a reward if he found the hat.

Max went searching and searched the entire circus grounds. Finally, he discovered a secret door in a corner of the square. When he opened it, he found himself in a mysterious cave filled with treasures and adventures.

But before he looked around, he saw the clown's magic hat and took it with him. But then he noticed that the cave was guarded by a huge, fire-breathing dragon.

Max, who was brave and smart, used his intelligence and found a way to defeat the dragon and escape. Back at the circus square, he handed the hat to the clown and got his reward. But he was happier that he had been able to help and that he had made his friends and family proud.

The moral of the story is that we should always help when someone is in need and that courage and intelligence can help us overcome any obstacle.

THE DISCOVERY OF THE wilderness

Once upon a time, there was a little boy named Max who loved to be out in nature. One day, he decided to go out on his own to explore the wilderness. With his backpack full of provisions and his compass, he began his journey.

It was a sunny day and Max wandered through the forest all morning. He saw birds, squirrels and rabbits and heard the sound of the river. As he walked along, it suddenly became darker and cooler. He knew he was going deeper into the forest and that he had to be careful.

As he looked around, he realized he couldn't find his way back. He was lost! But Max was not discouraged and continued on his way. Suddenly, he heard a strange noise and decided to follow it. It led him to a large, dark and dense bush. When he looked at it more closely, he discovered a cave.

Max decided to go into the cave and was fascinated by the darkness and coolness that surrounded him. When he turned around, he noticed something shiny in the darkness. It was a small jewel lying on the ground. Max knew he had found something very special and put the jewel in his pocket.

When he came out of the cave, he noticed that the sun was already setting and the forest was getting completely dark. Max knew that soon he would have to find a place to spend the night. Suddenly, he heard a loud roar and sensed something moving in the darkness. He was scared, but he remembered that he had to be brave.

Max turned on his flashlight and realized it was just a bear looking for food. He hid behind a tree and watched it. The bear moved on and Max was relieved. He found a place to spend the night and quickly fell asleep.

The next morning, Max found his way back and returned home. He was excited to tell all his adventures and proud that he was brave enough to explore the wilderness.

Max learned that sometimes you can get lost, but if you are brave and determined, you can find your way again. He also learned that you have to be careful in the wilderness and that it is important to be respectful of nature.

And so the story of Max and his adventures in the wilderness ended as he prepared for the next voyage of discovery, ready for all the adventures that life would offer him.

THE RACE OF THE RACE cars

It was a sunny day at the race track and all eyes were on the upcoming race. Young Max and his father have always been fans of race cars and were excited that this time they would get to be in a big race.

Max was sitting in the passenger seat when they reached the race car of the team his father worked for. The drivers were getting ready to compete and Max watched them with fascination. One of the drivers, Ben, came up to Max and his father and greeted them warmly. Max looked at him in awe, imagining what it would be like to sit in a race car himself and compete for victory.

The race began and Max and his father watched spellbound as the cars raced around the corners and an exciting head-to-head race developed. But suddenly Ben skidded and the car went off the track. Max and his father watched in horror as the car burst into flames.

But Ben did not give up. He fought his way out of the wreckage and ran back to the pit stop, where he immediately began preparing the reserve car for the race. Max and his father watched in fascination as Ben and his team quickly prepared the car and sent it back out on the track.

The race was now in full swing and Ben gave everything to catch up again. Max and his father cheered him on as he fought his way through the field and eventually moved up to second place. But first place seemed to be out of reach.

On the last lap, however, something unbelievable happened. The leading rider went off the track and Ben now had the chance to win the race. With incredible speed and precision, he overtook the remaining cars and finally crossed the finish line first.

Max and his father cheered with joy and admiration for Ben's courage and determination. They realized that racing is not only about speed and skill, but also about determination and the relentless pursuit of the goal.

They left the track that night with a valuable lesson they will never forget: The fighting spirit and determination to never give up can make the difference between winning and losing.

THE DAY ON THE FARM

It was a sunny day in spring when Max arrived at a farm with his family. Max was six years old and very excited because he had never been to a farm before. He couldn't wait to see and feed all the animals.

When they got out of the car, they heard the clucking of chickens and the bleating of sheep. Max saw a big red tractor driving through the fields, and he could smell the smell of fresh hay.

The family was greeted by a friendly farmer who showed them around and showed them all the animals. Max was especially impressed with the pigs playing in the mud and the cows grazing peacefully.

In the afternoon, the farmer told Max that he could help him feed the animals. Max was excited and took a bucket of corn to feed the chickens. When he entered the chicken coop, he noticed that a little chick had gotten lost and was not with its mother. Max knew he had to help.

He searched everywhere on the farm and finally found the little chick hiding under a bale of hay. It was hungry and very weak. Max took it to the mother cow and it drank milk and began to recover.

When the day ended, the farmer thanked Max for his help and gave him a little toy tractor. Max was so happy and proud to be able to help.

The moral of the story is that it is good to help others, especially animals that need our help. Sometimes all it takes is a little initiative and commitment to do something good.

The Enchanted Forest

Once upon a time there was a little boy named Max who was a great adventurer. One day he set off into the forest to have a new adventure.

As he ran deep into the forest, he realized he was lost. The forest suddenly looked completely different and he didn't know which way to go to find his way back home. But then he discovered something incredible: an enchanted forest!

Max could not believe it. The forest was full of colorful flowers and shining trees. Suddenly, he felt the forest come to life and he heard a voice telling him, "Welcome to the enchanted forest, Max. We've been waiting for you."

Max didn't know what to say. He was excited and a little scared at the same time. But then he saw a group of animals approaching him. They were animals he had never seen before: a fox with wings, a squirrel with a golden crown, and a rabbit with a magic wand.

They explained to him that the forest had been cursed by an evil wizard and they needed his help to break the spell and save the forest. Max was excited about the idea and agreed to help them.

They set off through the enchanted forest and met many magical creatures who helped them overcome obstacles and find their way. Together they fought against the wizard's evil creatures and finally they managed to break the spell.

The forest was saved and returned to its original beauty. The animals and creatures of the forest were grateful for Max's help and they decided to give him a special award: they named him Knight of the Enchanted Forest.

Max was overjoyed and proud of himself. But then he remembered that he had gotten lost and didn't know how to get back home. But the enchanted forest had a solution for that too: they gave him a compass that would always lead him in the right direction.

Max finally returned home safely and told his family and friends about his adventure in the enchanted forest. Not only had he saved the forest, but he had also learned that you should always listen to your heart and help others when you can.

THE DISCOVERY OF THE volcanic island

Once upon a time there was a little boy named Max who was a great fan of adventure and discovery. One day he read in a book about a volcanic island that had never been discovered by humans. Max couldn't resist and decided to go exploring himself.

He packed his backpack with provisions, water and equipment and set off for the volcanic island. When he arrived, he saw a beautiful yet frightening landscape before him: smoking volcanoes, hot springs and bubbling lava flows.

Max was not intimidated, however, and began his exploration. He discovered an abundance of rare plants and animals that existed nowhere else in the world. Suddenly, he heard a loud rumble and a volcano erupted. Max ran for his life and sought shelter in a cave.

When he thought he was safe, he realized he was not alone in the cave. A small frightened animal was sitting in a corner, shaking with fear. Max knew he had to help. He calmed the animal and together they looked for a way out of the cave.

Outside, however, another obstacle awaited them: another volcano erupted and lava flows blocked their way back to the boat. Max did not hesitate for a moment and used his equipment to build a bridge and bring the small animal safely across the lava flows.

After much hardship, Max finally returned home happy and proud. Not only had he explored the volcanic island and made many new discoveries, but he had also helped an animal in need and proved that courage and helpfulness are important.

So Max learned that discoveries and adventures can not only be exciting, but also lead us to overcome ourselves and help others. And who knows, maybe there are many more unknown islands and secrets waiting to be discovered by little adventurers like Max.

THE CONTEST OF THE wizards

Once upon a time, there was a small town where a wizards' contest was held every year. The children of the town were always excited and looked forward to this day. Max, a little boy of seven years old, was also especially excited. He had his heart set on winning the contest and earning the title of the best magician in town.

Max was a hardworking boy and had spent a lot of time learning and practicing new magic tricks. However, he had one problem - he was often insecure and nervous when performing magic in front of other people.

When the big day finally came, Max was more excited than ever. The stage was full of spectators and the other magicians were performing their best tricks. Max felt overwhelmed and wanted to run away.

But then he remembered his grandmother, who always told him to believe in himself and never give up. Max decided to gather his courage and show what he had learned.

He went on stage and started his magic trick. But suddenly something went wrong and all the audience laughed at him. Max was sad and wanted to give up.

But then he heard his grandmother's voice in his head: "Never give up, Max. Everyone makes mistakes, but it's important to learn from them and keep going."

Max decided to try again. He went on stage again and this time his trick worked. The audience was thrilled and Max had won the contest!

The moral of this story is that it is important to believe in yourself and never give up, even if you make mistakes. You can learn from mistakes and do better next time.

THE DAY AT THE AMUSEMENT park

It was a sunny day at the amusement park and Tim was excited because he would be riding all the roller coasters and carousels he could imagine. Along with his best friend Max and his family, he had come early in the morning and had the whole day ahead of him.

They started riding the roller coasters and it was so much fun, they felt like they could go on all day. But suddenly Tim realized that he had lost his cell phone. He searched all the pockets and asked his family if they had found it, but it was nowhere to be found.

Tim was very sad and scared. How could he find his family now if he was lost? He wondered if maybe he had lost his cell phone on one of the roller coasters.

He decided to look again for the last carousel he and his family had ridden together. When he finally found it, he discovered his cell phone on the floor under one of the seats. He was so relieved and happy that he cried out loud.

But then he saw that his cell phone was broken. He had apparently dropped it and the display was now completely destroyed. Tim was so sad that he almost cried.

But then he remembered something his grandfather had once told him: "Sometimes unforeseen things happen, but it's important how we deal with them. We should always try to make the best of every situation."

So Tim decided to make the best of the situation. He spent the rest of the day playing games with his family and having fun without worrying about his broken phone.

As they drove home at the end of the day, Tim felt happy and content. Even though he had lost and broken his phone, he had had a great day and had learned that sometimes it is important to make the best of a bad situation.

The moral of the story: sometimes unforeseen things happen, but it's how we handle them that matters. We should always try to make the best of every situation.

THE FIGHT AGAINST THE Yeti

Once upon a time, there was a little boy named Max who was incredibly brave and adventurous. One day he heard about a mysterious creature called Yeti who lived in the mountains and no one had ever seen him. Max was intrigued and decided to track down the Yeti and face him.

With a bag full of equipment, Max set off into the mountains. It was a long and dangerous way, but he didn't give up. When he finally reached the top, he saw a cave and knew that the yeti must be in there. He entered and suddenly found himself in a huge room full of ice and snow.

Suddenly he heard a noise and saw the Yeti coming towards him. Max was trembling with fear, but he remembered all the adventures he had already had and how brave he was in them. He faced the yeti and they fought an epic battle. But in the end, Max won by offering the yeti a friendship.

The yeti agreed and revealed his story to Max. He was a lonely yeti who was shunned by other animals because he looked different. Max realized that it was wrong to ostracize someone because of their appearance and that it was important to stand up for those who were different.

Max and the yeti became friends and Max helped him connect with other animals and build a community that valued everyone's differences. Max returned home and told his friends and family about his adventures and lesson learned. He was happy that he had found the yeti, but even happier that he had learned something that made him a better person.

The discovery of the ancient ruins

Once upon a time, there was a little boy named Max who was very enthusiastic about adventure and discovery. One day he set off into the jungle to search for hidden treasures and forgotten temples.

When he arrived in the deepest jungle, he discovered an ancient ruin. It was overgrown with wild grass and thick vines, but Max knew he had found exactly what he was looking for.

Full of curiosity and a sense of adventure, Max made his way into the ruin. He climbed over stones and walked through dark corridors until he finally discovered a secret chamber. Inside the chamber, he found an ancient scroll that was full of riddles and secrets.

Max was so excited that he wanted to solve the riddle right away. He pondered and thought until finally an idea came to him. He turned a secret switch and suddenly a hidden door opened.

Behind it, Max discovered a beautiful treasure consisting of sparkling gems and valuable artifacts. But before he could take the treasure, he heard a loud noise.

It was a group of wild animals roaming the jungle and moving towards Max. But Max was brave and ready to fight for his treasure. He grabbed a stick and faced the animals.

Thanks to his bravery and determination, Max was able to fight off the animals and secure his treasure. But on the way back to town, Max realized that he couldn't keep it all for himself. He decided to share some of the treasure with the people who lived in the jungle.

The people of the jungle were grateful for Max's generous gesture and welcomed him as a friend. Max learned that it was not only about discovering and winning, but also about sharing and helping.

Full of pride and joy, Max returned home and told everyone about his adventures and discoveries. People admired his courage and generosity and Max was happy to know that he had not only found a treasure, but had also made friends.

THE DREAM OF FLYING

Once upon a time there was a little boy named Tom who always dreamed of flying. Every evening he would look at the birds in the sky and wish that he could fly just like them. One day he decided it was time to make his dream come true.

He began by learning everything he could about flying. He read books, watched documentaries and even visited the nearby airport museum. One day he told his father about his dream and asked him if he could help him.

His father was a pilot and agreed to teach him everything he knew about flying. Together they built a small plane and spent weeks working on it and perfecting it.

Finally, the day had come when Tom would realize his dream of flying. He and his father got on the plane and took off. Tom couldn't stop smiling as he watched the earth get smaller and smaller as he climbed higher and higher into the sky.

But suddenly he heard a loud noise and the plane started to lurch. His father explained to him that they had run into turbulence, but that they had everything under control. Tom got scared, though, and wondered if he was really ready to fly.

When they finally landed safely, Tom was relieved that everything had gone well, but he was also disappointed that he couldn't fully realize his dream. However, his father explained to him that everyone who tries something new is scared, but it's important to keep going anyway. He also told him that it is okay to fail as long as you learn from it and try again.

Tom understood that it is okay to be afraid and that it is an important part of growing and achieving dreams. From that day on, he set a goal to continue learning and working hard to eventually achieve his dream of flying.

THE DAY AT THE AQUARIUM

It was a sunny day and Max couldn't wait to go to the aquarium. He had heard so much about all the fascinating creatures in the sea and he really wanted to see them with his own eyes. When he arrived with his family, he could hardly believe his eyes. All around him were huge tanks of colorful fish, starfish, crabs, and even sharks!

Max was so excited that he forgot about time and moved away from his family to explore even more. Suddenly, he noticed a mysterious door hidden in a secluded area of the aquarium. Max couldn't resist and opened the door. When he went inside, he discovered a huge tank that was almost as big as a swimming pool.

Max approached the tank and noticed something unusual. A small group of fish were swimming in a corner of the tank and moving strangely. Max realized they were trapped and trying to escape from the tank. He immediately understood that he had to help.

Max ran back to his family and told them about the trapped fish. Together they decided to inform the aquarium staff and help them free the fish. The aquarium staff was very grateful for Max's help and they were able to rescue the captured fish and relocate them to a larger tank.

Max was happy to see the rescued fish swim free. He realized that it was important to care for the environment and the creatures that live in it. Even though they were just small animals, saving them made a big difference.

As Max and his family left the aquarium, Max felt a warm sense of satisfaction and pride. He knew he had done something good and that it was important to care about the world around him.

The moral of the story is that everyone, no matter how small, can make a difference by helping others and caring for the environment.

THE SECRET MESSAGE

It was a sunny day and Tim and his friends were outside playing in the park. They were all excited because it was their last day before summer vacation and they had big plans for the next few weeks.

Suddenly, Tim spotted a strange note on the ground. He picked it up and saw that it was a secret message. The message was written in code, but Tim was a smart boy and he knew how to break codes. He showed the note to his friends and together they deciphered the message. It read, "Follow the map and find the treasure."

The children were excited and followed the map, which led them to an old abandoned house. They ventured inside and found another message that led them to a hidden park nearby.

There they found a box that contained an old key. They followed the next message, which took them to an abandoned building on the outskirts of the city. When they got there, they discovered a door that could be opened with the key.

Inside they found the treasure - a box full of candy and toys! The children were excited and began to share the treasure.

But then something caught Tim's eye. The box contained another message that read, "The real gift is the friendship and adventures you've shared together."

The children immediately understood that they had experienced the real gift of the day: having an adventure together and making friends. They hugged each other and looked forward to the upcoming summer vacation, when they would have even more exciting adventures.

And so Tim fell asleep that night happy and content, knowing that the true treasure of life is the people you share it with.

THE LOST TREASURE OF the Pharaohs

Once upon a time, there was a little boy named Tim who had heard about a legend of a lost treasure in the pyramids of Egypt. He was fascinated by the idea of finding a treasure and decided to plan an expedition to search for it.

Tim thought of a plan and set out. He traveled to Egypt accompanied by his parents and made his way to the pyramids. On the way there, he met an archaeologist named Dr. Smith who helped him plan his search.

They began their search in the largest pyramid and after a long search found a secret door that led to an underground room. There they found a map that showed the location of the treasure. However, the map was written in hieroglyphics, which Tim could not read.

They decided to find an expert who could help them translate the map. They found a famous archaeologist named Dr. Jones who assisted them and translated the map.

Tim and his team followed the map and eventually came to an ancient temple complex where they found a secret chamber. There they discovered a box with an inscription that said, "This treasure is not for those who seek it only for their own gain."

Tim realized that the treasure was not for him alone and decided to share it with others. They opened the box and found a collection of rare and valuable artifacts that had lain hidden for thousands of years.

They left Egypt with their treasure and decided to share it and show the world what they had found. Tim had learned that true treasure does not have to be only material and that it is more important to respect and share with others than to act alone.

After this adventure, Tim returned home, but he would never forget this unforgettable day in Egypt. He knew he had learned something important and looked forward to having more adventures in the future.

The Discovery of the Lost City

Once upon a time, there was a little boy named Tom who was always fascinated by adventure. One day he heard about a lost city hidden deep in the jungle, full of treasures and secrets.

Tom could hardly sleep for excitement and decided to go on his own voyage of discovery. He packed a backpack full of provisions and adventure gear and set off into the jungle.

After many days of wandering through dense brush and dangerous rivers, Tom finally discovered the ruins of an ancient city. He was excited and went into the city to explore.

Suddenly, he heard sounds of wild animals and quickly hid in one of the abandoned buildings. After a few minutes of silence, Tom ventured out again and continued his explorations.

He found a secret chamber where an old treasure map was hidden. The map showed the location of the city's lost treasure.

Tom was excited and determined to find the treasure. He followed the map deep into the jungle, through difficult terrain and dangerous obstacles. Finally, he reached a secret chamber where the treasure was located.

But when Tom touched the treasure, the earth began to shake and the walls started to crumble. Tom knew he had to act quickly to escape. He found a secret exit and ran as fast as he could while the city collapsed behind him.

Finally, Tom reached the end of the jungle and realized that adventures are not always about treasure and riches, but also about the thrill you experience when you take a risk and go beyond your limits.

Tom returned home feeling proud of himself for what he had accomplished. He knew that if he set his mind to something, he could accomplish anything.

The moral of this story is that adventure is not just about material rewards, but also about personal growth, courage and determination.

The mysterious forest

Once upon a time there was a boy named Max who, together with his friends, loved to play outside in the forest. They caught insects, built huts and played hide and seek. But one day they discovered a strange plant in the forest that they had never seen before. It was big and green and had thick, thorny leaves.

Max and his friends decided to get closer to the plant and suddenly saw that it was expanding into a forest. They decided to follow the trail to see where it led. Soon they found themselves in a mysterious forest filled with wondrous creatures and strange sounds.

While they were looking around, they suddenly heard a loud cracking sound. Max and his friends looked up and noticed a big shadow disappearing between the trees. They decided to follow it and finally came to an old hut inhabited by a mysterious man.

The man told them that the forest was enchanted and that it was their task to find the magical creature responsible for the spell. Max and his friends were excited and immediately set out to find the creature.

They wandered through the forest, fighting strange creatures and battling their own fears. Finally, they came to a small clearing where a glowing creature sat. It was the magical creature that had enchanted the forest.

Max and his friends were amazed at the beauty of the creature and how friendly it was. They talked to it and asked it to lift the spell so they could go back home. The creature agreed and told them to be careful not to leave the forest unattended again, as it was still full of dangers.

Max and his friends eventually returned home and told everyone about their adventure in the mysterious forest. They realized that sometimes you have to overcome fears to experience exciting things, but it's also important to heed warnings and stay safe.

And so that night, Max fell asleep happy and content, knowing that he and his friends had had an adventure they would never forget.

The battle against the giants

Once upon a time, there was a little boy named Tim who wanted nothing more than to be a great adventurer. One day he heard about a mysterious forest inhabited by giants. Tim was excited and decided to set out to find these giants.

When he arrived at the forest, Tim immediately noticed that he was not alone. He heard strange noises and sensed that someone or something was watching him. Suddenly he saw a shadow behind the trees, and when he got closer, he saw that it was a giant. Tim was scared, but he remembered his desire to be an adventurer and decided to keep going.

As he went deeper into the forest, he met more and more giants, all much bigger than him. Tim was so small and weak compared to them that he wondered if he even had a chance.

But Tim didn't give up. He was determined to find out what the giants were doing in the forest. One night he secretly watched the giants and discovered that they were removing a village from the forest and taking it to their own city. It was an incredible sight, and Tim knew he had to tell his friends.

He decided to go back to the town and ask for help. But when he reached the town, they laughed at him and called him a liar. But Tim did not give up. He knew what he had seen, and he knew he could prove it.

With the help of some brave friends, Tintin returned to the forest and fought the giants to bring back the stolen village. It was a difficult battle, but Tintin and his friends fought bravely. After a long and exhausting battle, they finally won against the giants.

When they brought back the village, Tintin was hailed as a hero. People realized that he had told the truth and admired his courage and determination.

The moral of this story is that if you believe in something, you should never give up, even if it is hard and others don't believe you. If you pursue your goals with determination and courage, you can achieve anything you want.

The adventures of the little dinosaur

Once upon a time there was a little dinosaur named Rex who lived in a beautiful landscape full of green forests and sparkling rivers. Rex was an adventurous dinosaur who was always on the lookout for new things.

One day, Rex heard about a fabled mountain where a great treasure was supposedly hidden. Rex was so excited that he decided to set out immediately to find this treasure. He packed his bag and set off.

The way to the mountain was not easy. Rex had to walk through a dense forest, jump over rushing rivers and climb steep mountains. But Rex didn't give up, he was determined to make his dream come true.

Finally, Rex reached the foot of the mountain. He climbed and climbed until he found the entrance to a cave. Rex entered the cave and noticed that the floor was shiny. It was the treasure he had been looking for!

But suddenly Rex heard a strange sound. It was the calls of a dangerous T-Rex that was also looking for the treasure. Rex knew he was in trouble, but he didn't give up. He knew he had to be brave to protect the treasure.

Rex and the T-Rex fought each other fiercely, but finally Rex managed to defeat the T-Rex. Rex had won, but he realized that it wasn't just about the treasure. It was also about courage and friendship. Rex understood that friendship and courage were just as important as treasure.

So Rex returned to his village a hero. He told his friends about his adventure and experiences and learned that the most important thing is to always be brave and kind, no matter what.

Impressum

LIOM LIOM
AUF DER HÖH 13A
35447 REISKIRCHEN
KONTAKT
E-MAIL: sl350sl@gmx.de

Don't miss out!

Visit the website below and you can sign up to receive emails whenever Liom Liom publishes a new book. There's no charge and no obligation.

https://books2read.com/r/B-A-AOUW-NLQGC

BOOKS 2 READ

Connecting independent readers to independent writers.

children. Let your kids immerse themselves in a world of adventure and fun and watch them fall asleep peacefully each night.

www.ingramcontent.com/pod-product-compliance
Lightning Source LLC
Chambersburg PA
CBHW020525160726
47992CB00016B/1241